BUSINESS
Credit Secrets
—— FOR ——
CHILDCARE SUCCESS

The ONLY way to PROTECT your BRAND and BUILD WEALTH

Asia L. Rivers

Copyright © 2018 (Talk Childcare To Me L.L.C.)

All rights to this book are reserved. No permission is given for any part of this book to be reproduced, transmitted in any form or means; electronic or mechanical, stored in a retrieval system, photocopied, recorded, scanned, or otherwise. Any of these actions require the proper written permission of the publisher.

Disclaimer

All erudition contained in this book is given for informational and educational purposes only. The author is not in any way accountable for any results or outcomes that emanate from using this material. Constructive attempts have been made to provide information that is both accurate and effective, but the author is not bound for the accuracy or use/misuse of this information.

First Printing: 2018
ISBN: 978-0-578-43703-3

P.O. Box 3732
Louisville, Ky 40201

Asia L. Rivers
Copyright © 2018

DEDICATION

For my sisters Niglah, Jamekia, and Korryn...
Keeping me grounded, as I found my way

TABLE OF CONTENTS

The Budding Entrepreneur 7

The Producer 19
Utilizing Your Business Credit 19

The Biz Credit Clean Up 35
Repairing, Restoring, or Reusing the Business Credit Profile 35

Protecting the business 41

Closing remarks 45

Credits & References 47

Note to the reader:

My credit journey is a continuing journey. You'll have one too, if you decide to grow or branch out. *Business Credit Secrets* is my guide for other childcare business owners who are stuck in the cycle of personal credit, business credit, personal guarantors, and cashflow holdups. This book targets how to build business credit, how to maintain it, how to grow it, and then how to manipulate the factors working against us. My area of expertise is childcare, but my niche is business credit.

Use this knowledge that's between these covers, to think outside the box. It can be challenging when we have to abide by all state and federal regulations and be in the public eye at every step. We weren't given a fund for retirement therefore we create one. Get ready for these business credit secrets that I'm about to unveil.

Let's get to the money!
Everybody Mad.

-O.T. Genasis

Someone tell me why business credit is such a secret. Why does an entrepreneur get penalized for making the jump into progressing their career? Creating jobs for families, establishing wealth for their own family, or simply making a living. This is exactly what I envisioned when I started my childcare business. What I didn't know about was the financial burden – just how much building my empire would cost. It cost me time with my family and several personal sacrifices, but it also hurt my credit. Everything I knew regarding credit came from hard lessons and proper research. We've all experienced hardships with credit. But mine were filled with endless collection calls (before it was illegal), maxed credit cards, unpaid medical copays, unpaid cell phone bills, and even repossessions. As quickly as I possessed my brand-new car based on my wages from a 9 to 5, it was quickly removed due to my 1099. Afterwards, I had a bright idea to clean up my credit and start researching/building business credit. Little did I know my personal credit, assets, cash, and savings would be put through the wringer while running a business. It was a round of the *Hunger Games*.

Like many aspiring entrepreneurs, I didn't understand the basics of business credit. One quick search on Google gave me all the information I needed, or so I thought. I searched for things like "How personal credit fits with business credit", "Funding for small business", "Small business lending without collateral", "Business loans for people with bad credit", "Running a business with bad credit." Now, let me be honest and say my score wasn't terrible but it wasn't "The 700 Club" either. I thought working three jobs and paying everything with cash would lessen the amount I'd pay out once I was approved for a small business loan. The harder I worked, the less time I spent on growing the business side of my childcare business. I had less time to continue researching ways to perfect my business establishment. Many people do not know the difference between business credit and personal credit. I was one of them. I ordered stuff from the internet with my business name, paid for them, and patted myself on the back for doing what I thought was right. I was operating as a consumer and not a merchant. The moment I became an owner, it was time to play a larger game. Regardless of how small I was, my focus had to be all about the business, and I had to operate like a Fortune 500 company.

Once I started my business, it grew pretty quickly. My space was small, and I outgrew our initial capacity within six months. I was forced to try and expand. I was in a city filled with childcare needs but lacked consistent cashflow, business savings, and sufficient working capital for an expansion. My initial thought was, let's go to a bank… the rejection still echoes in my ear.

Me:

No, What do you mean no?

But I've worked from sun up until sun down.

I've missed my kid's functions.

I was sick……

My husband was sick…..

Business Banker:

"Well ma'am, you need business credit and collateral to compliment your application for business credit. Your business doesn't have a business credit score, and your personal credit is being used for the application."

In deep thought:

Aaaaaahhhhh…..Business credit…only for the prestigious business owner, right?

I would sit and wonder, what's the difference between my business and another business. Is my status of being a business owner any less than the next? Upon researching, I discovered the difference could be measured as an 80 Paydex score. My goal of expanding diminished rapidly due to my lack of knowledge. The importance of establishing business credit didn't dawn on me until I maxed out all my personal credit for business purchases.

Business Banker:

"After the review, it isn't quite what we would consider a favorable score. Do you have anyone who's willing to co-sign or do you have any assets to pledge?"

Still in deep thought:

Pllleeeaasse...apparently you haven't seen the credit scores of my kin. Hell, my score is the cream of the crop. All of a sudden, it feels like an episode of *The Twilight Zone*. My home, my family, my center, my staff, and the children lie in jeopardy.

"Naw," I responded. I'm thinking, how many other hoops do I need to jump through to obtain funds? This woman continues to stare at me as I'm staring at her. "What about my business plan? I pay the center's bills on time...isn't that good enough?"

As a childcare owner, there's nothing worse than wanting to provide a safe and healthy location for children but can't due to lack of resources. I needed quality furniture for my center, a decent center van, and cashflow to pay my bills on time. The pressure for quality wasn't a want, it was my standard. The low-income families had nearly doubled our capacity within a month. The clientele was present but immediate access to cash and materials wasn't.

Business Banker:

"At this time, Mrs. Rivers, your application has been denied based off the current information received. Your denial notices will be mailed to you. If you have any questions about any of the information we used in our decision, call the number on the letter. We look forward to serving our customers here at ....so and so (done listening) bank."

Shit....and there I was. One year in, pregnant with our third child, at capacity, no money, and pawning or selling everything in sight to feed my vision, and our family. The hardest thing I've ever had to do was make the decision to hand over my wedding ring for our family to eat. I've never been a quitter. Determined…. always, but never a quitter.

Most people would stop right there. Even my husband and I were at odds as to where the fate of the center would lay. I'd pray, he'd pray, and we would coast right back into our regular flow. But my vision remained the same. I knew I wanted to grow, but I didn't know how. From that moment, I started applying for business lines of credit with a personal credit score of 640. I applied for any account that contained the words "Business Credit."

The never-ending cycle of denials were like knives in my back. All I could hear was judgment being passed as a gavel echoed. I was denied, and denied, and denied. I had my personal credit checked repeatedly in a short period of time, and it counted against me. My inquiries doubled within just 30 days—36 inquiries, to be exact. This was primarily because I didn't understand the inner workings of business credit and how it affected personal credit. By approaching it this way, I only did myself an injustice. I received denial notices for a range of reasons: high industry rating risk, past delinquent personal credit history of a guarantor, inability to verify the business address, and lack of established business credit. I was stuck, and I lacked the financial potential to grow beyond my current center. But there's one thing about opportunity—it doesn't stay open for long. So, as the business owner, what do you do about business credit? At that moment, I decided not to be another statistic. Not to be another failing, black owned, woman-owned, and small business. It was time to boss up my mentality. My center wouldn't become one of those businesses struggling to make it. God was on my side. He sent me water and the cleansing process began. Out with the old information and in with the new.

I went looking for credit in all the wrong places. I'd apply for credit at major banks that I had no previous history with. I explored all business credit products that were available. Cashflow credit lines, business credit cards, gas cards, commercial real estate products, and the list continues. Each product had its own uniqueness and specific qualifications and I was shot down. My personal score was in the high 600's and the world's telling me, "Asia, you should be eligible for credit.... just not business credit, though." The world was staring and making assumptions about how, I was a business owner with bad credit and no business credit. I was consistently denied. Driven by entrepreneurial spirit, I'm not the type of person that accepts being told no. I will not accept no for an answer. Just because one person tells you no doesn't mean there's not an opportunity to have a yes. So, I began to create my own tracking system upon researching business credit.

Strive not to be a success But rather to be of value

-Albert Einstein

THE BUDDING ENTREPRENEUR

Deciding to open a business is a BIG decision. The moment you decide to leap, you become all about the business. Being a business owner, your work priorities have to come first. Your personal credit is the gateway to business credit. You cannot skip the steps of maintaining reasonable personal credit (600+) and building pristine business credit. Know that all things are possible, and you've got this. Due to the big banks' financial crisis from 2004-2010, most business lenders require a personal guarantee. Some may remove the personal guarantee from your personal credit file if the account has a long-standing, positive credit history, but most likely not. If you don't have a credit score anywhere near a 600, start pulling copies of your credit report. The government allows every person one free copy from each credit bureau annually. Simply Google "Free Annual Credit Report". You will be able to access your personal credit reports from the Transunion, Equifax, and Experian credit bureaus.

Accessing these three consumer reporting agencies will give your business a lifeline. The lifeline will only come in handy if you've proven yourself within the past two years. Proving yourself is defined as making on-time payments, keeping credit card balances relatively low (under 30% utilization), and having a substantial amount of available credit. If you have some credit issues, try paying down high balances on credit cards, disputing inaccurate items, and paying accounts on time. These things will help your score skyrocket to the next level. If you need some help disputing collection items, a free resource called Collection Shield 360 could be an option. Collection Shield 360 may assist in sending legal documents to collection accounts if you disagree with information on your credit report. Also, the dispute process to get items corrected or verified is called the 609 process. It's also important to add that you may still owe the debt even after it's been removed from your credit report. You may also use an agency, but there's plenty of free credit help available online. Find one that fits your budget. Time, consistency, and paperwork is of the essence when disputing items displayed on your credit report.

In order to learn about business credit, we must know what it is, and the brief history associated with it. Afterwards, we'll begin to understand why it's such a secret to the public and how you can begin to tap into the business credit world and utilize it. Building business credit will create access to traditional funding without having to secure a co-signer or put up collateral. These are the types of things that aren't taught in traditional business courses.

What is Business Credit?

Business credit is the exchange of goods and/or services from business to business. A business credit score is the measurement at which the business is likely to pay. Business credit can also be defined as a form of trade between a business and creditors, often referred to as trade lines. These trade lines may be monetary (in the form of loans) or goods and products sold. The amount of business credit available is based on the business's financial health.

Why do you need business credit?

Business credit was created to maintain separation of personal and business finances. Not only is intermingling of funds frowned upon by the IRS, but it's a nightmare to sort through if you ever try to get approved for a large purchase, such as a car or home. The separation comes in the form of a Tax Identification Number (TIN) that's tied to the business. Just like your social security number is tied to you. Both numbers are unique and must be safeguarded. If you're going global, you'll need an international tax identification number. Be sure contact your local office tax office for details. If you're outside the U.S., contact the local at U.S. embassy. If the business lacks credit, you run the risk of becoming personally liable for credit accounts. Ask yourself: would a bank loan you money today, based on your previous financial decisions? If you don't have at least a 700-credit score, a traditional bank will not loan money for a business without collateral.

Business startups are considered very risky when it comes to lending. So, get used to hearing the word "no". Even with a credit score of 700, you'll have to personally guarantee the loan as well. A personal guarantee is when you become personally liable for the loan should business cease. The majority of the time, the credit line will be reported on your credit report even if it's a business loan. If you decide to personally guarantee the account, a bank will require a credit score minimum of 600. Anything less (even 598) will cause problems. This typically results in loans that have high interest rates. Again, these types of loans can be daunting, and the bank is ensuring it gets its money back, but you have to decide if that's what's best for you and your business. Again, never start a business on loan.

Who plays a part in the Business Credit arena?

The main three business credit bureaus:

- Dun and Bradstreet: measures company risk through a Paydex Score
- Experian Business Solutions: measures business and supplier risk
- Equifax Small Business: measures primarily business risk

In comparison to Personal Credit Scores, how does it differ from Business Credit?

Personal credit is measured normally on a scale of 300 (high risk)-850/900 (low risk) depending on which scoring algorithm is used. Each consumer credit bureau will differ in its scoring guide depending on the type of credit and the year of the scoring model. Business credit ranges on a scale of 0 (high risk/high failure) - 100 (anticipated payment/ low failure risk). Business credit scoring models do not fluctuate, and they're consistent across each business credit bureau unless supplied information is incorrect or altered.

How do I get started building?

Get Established.

It's important to know what your role will be before you get established. Either you're just going to be the owner, you're going to be the owner/director, or you're going to be in partnership with someone else.

These roles should be clearly defined, researched, and maybe even job shadowed before you get established. Getting established means deciding how your business is going to be structured. Are you going to be a sole proprietor, meaning that you're the sole business owner? Being a sole proprietor means everything's attached to your social security number. Or what about a limited liability company (LLC)? If you're an in-home center and you are working for yourself, then it's probably best to remain a sole proprietor, because it's just you. Being taxed as an L.L.C. may not be in your best interest. The moment you want to go larger, you'll need to restructure and adjust your current business to carry over into your future. Think of it as a bridge. Everyone's situation is different depending on their unique vision. Getting established as an LLC provides the separation between yourself and the business. It gives you limited protection should something go wrong with your business, meaning that you still have your name (Doing Business As) and not your business name attached to it. The main three business classifications are sole proprietorship, corporations, or partnerships. There are pros and cons based on your business type, owner(s), and how large the company is. Talk to your CPA, tax attorney, and bookkeeper to make a sound decision.

Another business classification is non-profit, for-profit, or not- for-profit. Each classification has its pros and cons, but this classification mainly involves the way you fund the business, how you pay people, tax responsibilities, and who gets what during closure. In order to make an informed decision, decide how big you want to start. Do you want to have employees? If so, will you be able to afford payroll taxes? Be sure to visit the IRS website for questions related to each business setup and which payroll taxes you'll be responsible for. Do not make the mistake of paying wages and the decision to not pay payroll taxes (trust fund taxes) and/or filing untimely returns. Uncle Sam will place a lien on your business and levy your bank accounts if it's not received.

Be sure to establish a game plan with an accountant and an attorney so that you can remain protected. Explain your vision, as well as the resources available to you, and they will help you make an informed decision about choosing your business organization setup. You will need to rely on their expertise so choose wisely. If you don't know where to start, Google Dave Ramsey. He has many financial principles and resources for you to soak up. Some resources are free while others aren't. We all have to operate within a budget, but always remember to take advantage of every opportunity to retain the knowledge. Dave Ramsey has a CPA-Endorsed Local Provider (ELP) listing for your area. This listing is comprised of CPAs that have been examined and monitored. Choose one and choose wisely.

The last determining factor will be how you make money. For example, if you are a for-profit center, you are virtually eliminated from all grants. Now, it is possible to go through another sponsoring nonprofit organization to acquire a grant, but the organization normally requires a contract of commitment from all owners involved. Being established as a non-profit will exempt your business from paying some payroll taxes. Every business's tax situation is unique which is why it's worth looking into a CPA. For example, my business is Rivers Educational Center, LLC. On a state level, I'm recognized as an LLC but the federal government doesn't recognize my business as an LLC due to it being a single-member LLC. As the sole owner, all of my business dealings will be filed as a schedule C on my tax return. Filing a profit results in additional tax due. Filing a loss may be a perceived benefit but creditors that ask for your tax return may see a loss and deny credit. The best way to avoid the pitfall is to consult a CPA.

On a side note, my trade name is Rivers Educational Center. I've trademarked my logos and name for a small price. No one can take my business name or logos associated with it. For those of us who use design websites, these designs cannot be trademarked. So, hire a designer and be unique. If you're unable to trademark your name, write down dates to confirm how long you've had the name and logos. It may come into question later if someone decides to use it. Just because you haven't trademarked it doesn't mean someone can claim it. You may not be able to issue a cease and desist without the paper trail, but no one has the right to take what's not theirs. To file for monetary damages, you have to register the trademark beforehand. Again, consult a trademark and copyright attorney for specific details pertaining to your situation.

Once you're organized as a business at the state level, you can start the process of applying for a federal tax ID number, better known as an employer identification number (EIN or TIN). Apply for an EIN by mail, telephone, fax, or online. Online is the quickest, and it provides documentation instantly when requirements are met. Simply visit the IRS website for information. Remember, applying for an EIN will allow you to open a business bank account. Concerning your bank account, when payments are received via check or money order, they must be written to the correct party. If the name used for the payment is incorrect, it will slow up the depositing of your money and the availability of your funds. If you think the business organization setup is tricky, hire a professional who is locally based. There are a lot of do-it-yourself tactics, but if errors are made, you may have to restart the clock on building business credit. Something as simple as a wrong street address can screw up business credit building.

Here is the 10-Step Business Strategy Guide. Read the guide and refer back to it often. Many mistakes are made if one step isn't executed correctly.

1.) Each state has its own process when establishing an organization of business. Most filings are referred to as "Articles of Organization". If you've managed to get established in business without being properly organized, then make it official. You cannot get a business bank account or even a merchant ID without this type of state filing.

2.) All business addresses have to match and remain consistent. While getting established, make sure your business address is an exact match across all paperwork. If your Articles of Organization paperwork spells the business address as "Street" then you must also apply for credit with the exact spelling. Do not vary spelling as this could result in two different credit profiles. The goal is to have one strong profile with little or no variations.

3.) Apply for an Employer Identification Number (EIN). You can apply at www.irs.gov or by mail. Do not proceed without an EIN. Ensure that the Articles of Organization paperwork (name) matches with the same business name on the IRS EIN paperwork. Make sure to store your EIN document in a safe place.

4.) Apply for a Dun and Bradstreet number at http://www.dnb.com. The process could take up to 30 days. Dun and Bradstreet could call to verify business information so be available for the call.

5.) Establish a business bank account in the business name. When applying at a bank, they will ask for your Business TAX ID/EIN, a copy of your Articles of Organization, and a copy of your Driver's License/Identification. If the business contains partners, all parties will have to be present for signing the documentation. Also, start to pay expenses for the business from the business account. If you have the opportunity to pay online, process some payments as EFT/ACH Debit. You will need the business routing and account number.

6.) Research each major small business credit bureau. Type in each bureau in Google. Make sure to read the FAQ's section.

- Dun and Bradstreet
- Equifax Small Business
- Experian Small Business

7.) Track your payments and spending with vendors. Make a list of all creditors or trade payments made from the business account. Place a check mark in the column in which the vendor reports. If you don't know, simply look at a statement and call the creditor. Ask for their credit department. Place the information into a spreadsheet as shown in the example below:

	D&B	Equifax Small Business	Experian Small Business
Rent			
Business Credit Card			
Fuel Card			
Corporate Account			

8.) Review and have some type of business credit monitoring in place. Some websites such as NAV are free, but the information can be delayed. You can also set up credit monitoring directly with each bureau for monthly or annual pricing. Be sure the method fits your business budget and assists with your credit goal.

9.) Plot your credit game plan. The goal is to identify which companies will report and how often. The more creditors you have reporting, the more your business credit grows. Figure out how many creditors are reporting and how many more you'll need to achieve your credit goal.

10.) Create your credit playbook. Your game plan will be the first part of your credit playbook when acquiring business lines of credit. The first round of business credit building requires at least six trade payments to be made in a timely manner to each credit bureau. If the account is Net 30, then you must pay BEFORE the 30th day/due date. Every day counts when building business credit.

What vendors do I start with?

If you do not have a business credit score, it simply means the business hasn't been registered correctly or vendors have not reported payment experiences. For a score to be generated, you'll need a minimum of four to six reporting vendors. Here are a few vendors/creditors which I used. These companies will help you gain immediate access to reported trade lines. Those vendors are:

- SPRINT Business Cellphone Service
- Quill
- Uline

Apply with your business Tax ID, with the correct address as shown on your Articles of Organization document, and the exact spelling of the business name. The game of business credit is to pay when the invoice has been received. Anything outside the net terms is recorded as slow payments, which will lower the overall business score. The more reporting vendors, the less of an impact. And vice versa, the less reporting vendors, the more of an impact it will make. If you need more assistance, the Biz Credit Directory is available for purchase at www.TalkChildcareToMe.com.

With Uline.com, you can establish your business account, and you can order supplies. Even though you're just starting out, start small. Order a box of paper which is 5,000 sheets of paper. It costs you about $30. Or you can order some other items, but for this to make an impact, the final order has to total over $50. You order $50 worth of product, and every quarter, Uline will report to Experian and Equifax. That will start to build your business credit. Make sure you pay it on time, because if you don't pay it on time, meaning every 15 days, they'll start reporting late or missed trade payments. You don't want to rack up missed trade payments. It's bad for business, and you don't want to start off on the wrong foot.

Your relationships with people will determine the type of person you will attract and the type of business that you'll keep. As an owner, you'll have to prescreen clientele because they can be your downfall. You most definitely don't want a center of clients that come in, receive services, and fail to pay. This is the same with business credit. Business creditors don't want to do business with other businesses if they cannot pay within the stated terms. They have cashflow and overhead as well. In order to alleviate the extra expense of overhead and increase their profit margins, you may see a price markup on their products. These suppliers/vendors have an added overhead for credit bureau reporting. It's a significant cost to sustain accurate business credit data. The lower the business credit score, the higher the risk. In the beginning you'll eat those costs to start business credit building.

You're responsible for paying your staff and, if your parents don't make the payments when they're scheduled to be made, you still need to pay the bills. If you can't make this happen, this is not the business for you. Your business thrives off good credit and how you handle those client/credit obligations. It's much worse than your personal credit but again, your business credit starts off from your personal credit, and the business will begin to mold its own credit. Think of the business as a child. A child doesn't have any credit and so where do they get credit from? If you ask other affluent families, they all would tell you to add them as an authorized user in order to build their credit. If they don't have any credit starting off, they can't obtain any credit easily. The business starts off being an authorized user on your personal credit until it establishes its own. Take care of your business and it will take care of you.

The process could take about 90-120 days once you see those accounts actually reporting. I didn't have a lot of money. And most people working in the child care industry don't. Upon completion of four to six reporting vendors, you will have completed round one of business credit building. Round 1 heavily focuses on trade payments. Normally, office supplies, equipment, furniture, etc. These types of trade lines are useful if your main objective is to stretch your cashflow. For example, my program was largely funded by the state, therefore a large source of our revenue came once a month. I often needed supplies before I got paid. Utilizing my business credit through vendors allowed me to keep operating without having to borrow money. I didn't become cashflow broke by using all of my cash on hand. Working in childcare, we often face unexpected expenses, and they don't come at a cheap price. You never want to tell a contractor you don't have the money or worse, close the business due to cashflow (only). Once you build a solid score of an 80, it's time to get the money to place business dealings on autopilot.

Below is sample of a spreadsheet I used to start tracking:

	D&B	Equifax Small Business	Experian Small Business
Sprint Service	+ (Net 30)	-	+
Quill	+ (Net 30)	-	+
Uline	+ (Net 30)	-	+
Corporate Account	+ (Net 55)	+	-

Simplicity is the ultimate sophistication.

-Leonardo DaVinci

THE PRODUCER

Utilizing Your Business Credit

The thing that pained me the most was operating a childcare center and keeping up with the extreme amount of mail from invoices due. Then I had to coordinate how I was going to pay each bill before the due date, and if my state payment was late…. all hell broke loose. I got tired of picking up the phone to call 15 vendors, to tell them I couldn't pay that day but in two days I'd be able to. In addition, the money is often spent by the time it hits your bank account. This phenomenon is called being "cashflow broke". I can't pay today but I can next week. It's the business equivalent of living paycheck to paycheck. That cashflow makes the business world go around. Expenses have to be paid, the most important of which is payroll. No one wants to work for someone if they can't get paid on time. In order to alleviate these problems, I dove a little further into utilizing my business credit.

In Round 2, it's a more challenging. This round deals with serious money not materials. The terms are more stringent, and the challenge is to weigh the risk of having your personal credit pulled for a business account. BUT wait a minute! I know what you're saying – I thought the purpose of business credit was to keep it separated. However, creditors want to know if the business owner is committed to paying the debt back. This is the reason to avoid being a business owner with bad credit. A lot of people think that it's okay – "If I have business credit, they never will check my personal credit." False. Creditors will check personal credit and use it as a pre-qualifier. A decision will be made based off the credit check. You're acting as the parent organization during the business credit building process. Somethings to keep on mind, even though you might not put your social security number on a credit application for your business, some creditors and banks will still run a soft pull on your credit. The only way to know this, is if you have credit monitoring either through Credit Karma or Credit Sesame. I'm just naming some of the free credit monitoring agencies that people most commonly use. You won't know that they have checked it in conjunction with your business credit unless you're paying attention. When I was at Round 2, I had Credit Karma, Credit Sesame, and MyFico monitoring my personal credit. It may seem overboard, but in order to level up, you'll need to use the Boss Up Mentality (B.U.M.)

Which means, when others go low you go high, and with class. You may have perfect business credit, but if the personal credit score is lower than 600, you won't be approved. Let's take a closer look at Round 2 business credit.

What types of business credit are there?

-Revolving (Credit Cards)
-Installment (Business Loan, Store Card)
-Money/Revenue-Based Loans
-Leases

What if there's incorrect information?

When information is incorrect on your business credit profile, it can damage the score and leave you feeling discouraged. The best plan of action is to contact the credit bureau directly and initiate a dispute. A business credit bureau dispute is not like a personal credit file dispute. In addition, each bureau has their own unique way of disputing the information. Note: when reading the report, you will not be able to see the name of the creditor, only the listed industry; unless you request for the name to be unveiled. This is an additional process. The creditor has the right to deny the name disclosure. When I viewed my report for the first time, I noticed a $250 charge from a company. The last reporting date was from 2015. It was a three-step process to get it removed. Not to mention the company closed due to bankruptcy. Another instance was a cellphone company that reported. The industry was listed as a retail store and not radio telecommunications. I tried to dispute, no change occurred, and they would not release the name. However, they eventually sent an invoice. It was 100 bucks, which was debt beyond terms (DBT). I paid, and they updated the report. But again, I didn't know anything about business credit, and it was counted against me until I walked through the proper process. Each business credit reporting agency has a different dispute method. In order to dispute reported information, you'll have to call each agency and request their specific dispute form. This process is unlike the 609 process from personal credit reporting.

Can I make minor changes on my credit profile?

Regarding Dun and Bradstreet, I can look up any business, and anyone can have access, for a substantial fee. You can search any business's name and their Dun and Bradstreet number. You can't go any further than that unless you want to purchase a premium product for a premium price, but you can do that, if you choose. Also, if you have a Dun and Bradstreet number already, you can pull up your company update, and you can automatically see who's reporting to your credit report without actually having to pay a premium price. Definitely a money-saving tip without the hassle. Childcare owners love to save money. I know I do, and I know I don't have money to spend just to see my credit score or act on something I know nothing about. Here's an example of what to expect from a Dun and Bradstreet Company Update (Exhibit A) :

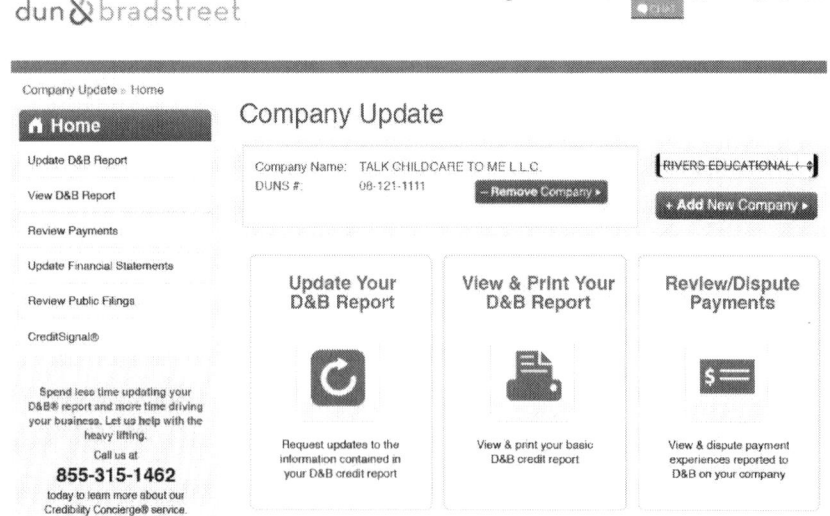

Exhibit A

When logging onto Dun and Bradstreet's site (Exhibit A), search for your company; you'll see if a company update is available. Enter in all correct information that's specific to your business. If you can't find your company, it's possible you may not have a D&B file. If not, cancel and follow the steps in the 10-Step Strategy Guide.

This company update will show you what changes will need to be made on the credit reports. It shows increases and decreases, and even consistency of payment history. So, you can receive free updates to your D&B scores and ratings if you want, but you can always go to your company update and again, it's accessible for free. So those of you who don't know whether or not something's reporting to your credit bureau, here's a free, easy way to know if it is or not. I began to create my own tracking system on how to build business credit within less than 90 days. It was an easier transition; the only options that you can find online are big corporations that try to sell you on business credit and promise they can get you thousands, or even millions, of dollars for your small business for upwards of $2500.

Take the scenic route and know business credit. Being a business owner doesn't apply to only one business. Create multiple streams with credit options that you decide. Cash is King, and Credit is Power. These companies either build it, or they don't. It's a crap shoot I'm not willing to take. There are enough odds against us in this business – cuts to child care subsidies, declines in enrollment, cost of insurance, and lack of health benefits. We love our childcare industry, but the business of childcare does not love us. Build a strong foundation of knowledge, and you could pass it along and create generational wealth. Do not waste your time and money on scams. Easy come and easy go.

You told us the address is important

The street address is crucial, especially when you're getting established. You have to make sure that the street address, your business name, and all other business info matches up or you'll end up with two credit profiles for one business. It happened to me. My address was listed as 1156 South 6th Street instead of 1148 South 6th Street. Same business name. I had another account that listed my business name as Rivers Educational Center, LLC but I also had another credit account that listed the business as Rivers Educational Center L.L.C. when getting established, the business name and the business address are spelled exactly the same, and consistent with what's listed on the articles of organization and/or the federal tax ID paperwork. Accuracy counts. In addition, sometimes people make mistakes, and it's human error. The administrative staff inputting your information may just type it in wrong. And you the business owner don't reap any benefits from that. In either case – be it a processing error or your mistake – you've got two different credit profiles and the creditor, who's determining if you'll be awarded credit, may be looking at a different profile. And it could be old, it could be new. It could be all over the place. It may sound unlikely, but it happens, go back and cover your bases.

In addition to multiple credit profiles, the account could be tagged as fraudulent. Even if there's a verifiable change. But everything is a process. In order to initiate an address change, you'll backtrack and start at the secretary of state via the Articles of Organization, notify the IRS of the address change, and then accounts/credit bureaus. If you don't follow the order, you risk the integrity of the account and account closure.

Denial Letters

Oh, the pain of denial letters. Let's take a look at a few I received.

Ally Bank
PO BOX 1048
HARTFORD CT 06143

RIVERS EDUCATION CENTER
1148 S 6TH ST
LOUISVILLE, KY 40203

June 20, 2017

1-877-401-2559
Application Number 1057740646

Co-Applicant Asia Rivers

This will acknowledge receipt of your request for the specific reasons which influenced our response concerning whether we would be prepared to accept your obligation if the credit sale or lease of a 2014 FORD ECONOLINE WAGON or other product to you was completed by D.J. Leasing Llc, 6507 Preston Hwy, Louisville, KY, 40219-1819.

In making our credit decision, we used a credit scoring system to assist us. The system assigns points to some of the items of information in your application, your credit history, and credit bureau reports on you.

We were not agreeable to handling the proposed transaction for the following reasons:

- Credit bureau score based on your credit report - see reasons below - Co-Applicant
- Credit Bureau score too low – Applicant
- Too many credit bureau inquiries in last 6 months – Applicant
- Amount to be capitalized or financed excessive in relation to vehicle value

The information included the following significant factors:

- Serious delinquency (Co-Applicant)
- Time since delinquency is too recent or unknown (Co-Applicant)
- Level of delinquency on accounts (Co-Applicant)
- Too many inquiries last 12 months (Co-Applicant)

Exhibit B

Now the task is left up to the business owner to become a detective, and you have to be the snoop, and search out and research exactly what's on that letter. Not only did the creditor use my personal credit history as a co-applicant, they used my business credit as well. Therefore, they used both of them together, to make a credit decision. Not huge issues but look at the incompleteness of my business name, my business credit score was too low (not enough trade-lines established), too many business credit inquiries, vehicle purchase price is too high, and not to mention my overall personal credit issues at that time.

AMAZON.COM
P.O. Box 965055
Orlando, FL 32896-5055
1-866-634-8381

June 20, 2017

RIVERS EDUCATIONAL CENTER LLC
ATTN: A RIVERS
1148 SOUTH 6TH STREET
LOUISVILLE, KY 40203

Account Number Ending In: 2373
Dear Commercial Customer,

Synchrony Bank has received your credit line increase request for your AMAZON.COM account. We are unable to approve your request at this time.

The reason(s) for our decision are listed below:

Insufficient credit experience

Some information used to make this decision was obtained from the credit reporting agency listed below. This credit reporting agency did not make this credit decision and is unable to provide you with the specific reason(s) for our action. If you believe there may be information on your credit report that is not correct, we suggest you contact the credit reporting agency below to verify the information.

Dun & Bradstreet
Attn: Customer Service
3501 Corporate Pkwy
PO Box 520
Center Valley, PA 18034
Telephone: 1-800-234-3867

If you have any questions or if we may be of further assistance, please contact us on-line or at the toll free number above.

Exhibit C

On my denial letter, I applied for an Amazon Commercial Credit increase. If you're not familiar with what type of account, that's a commercial credit account, and it's revolving, so it acts as if it's an online credit card. I can't spend it in a regular store; I can only spend it with Amazon. When I first started applying for business credit, I didn't know this, so I just basically ran my social security number and my business credit numerous times, and it got counted against me. When applying for the line of credit, Amazon pulls Equifax only. I was only doing an injustice to myself. Within my first three years of business, I had over 36 credit inquiries just because I didn't understand the innerworkings of business credit and how it affected personal credit. Obtaining the Net 55 account through Amazon skyrocketed my business credit and allowed flexibility to grow and obtain big ticket items for my center. I was able to purchase commercial appliances, order quality supplies for classrooms, and ease my cashflow issues. I didn't need a loan from a large bank, and the account wasn't attached to my personal credit. After a year, I requested an increase but was denied. On that denial letter, (Exhibit B) it states, that the business has **insufficient credit experience**. Meaning that I do not have enough reporting tradelines to increase my limit. They used Dun and Bradstreet in their decision. The easy fix is to create more relationships with vendors/creditors and/or establish credit references. Usually, the recommended credit rating is referred to when deciding to grant credit limit increases.

Another common reason for credit denial (D & B) is the industry rating risk. There's nothing more frustrating than someone not wanting to do business because you've been credit profiled. The creditor perceives too much risk due to other businesses classified as daycares or childcare centers. The failure rate of childcare centers is also a key factor. This is the main reason some property owners will not rent for the purposes of operating a childcare center. As a suggestion, use another NAICS code that is applicable (more favorable) or try another vendor/creditor to work with. Equifax Small Business works the same way, but you also want to pay attention to your industry risk rating. Your industry risk rating is going to make or break you. Regardless of how strong your credit score is, both personal and business, if your industry risk rating score is substantially low, you'll less likely to obtain business credit. The creditor's going to look at you as high risk. In addition, the childcare industry as a whole has a higher risk rating compared to other industries.

The NAICS code is tied to your business credit but also census data. These are your federal codes that are specifically tied to your business. In my case, with Talk Childcare to Me, my code is "business consulting, other management consulting services". Dig further you'll see childcare services on Rivers Educational Center. Need to change or update your NAICS? This is information found through the Dun and Bradstreet company update – a free resource. If you need more information on NAICS codes, search NAICS on the census website.

What are the main Business Credit Monitoring Agencies?

-Nav (FREE)
-Experian ($20 - $149)
-Equifax ($20 - $149)
-Dun & Bradstreet ($199 - $1,800)

Before we dive into more specifics about the business credit agencies, let's cover some basic payment terms. When reviewing your invoice, you may see "N" which stands for net terms. Depending on the creditor terms vary. Common terms are net 30, net 60, or net 90. NET is simply referred to when the payment is due to the creditor. Go past those terms and payments become DBT or Debt Beyond Terms. Exceeding net terms will have a direct impact on your business credit score. Never fear, DBT isn't the hardest situation to pivot.

With most creditors they're looking to see your personal credit in the green at Round 2. A personal credit score of 700 combined with a Dun & Bradstreet score of 75-80 is usually an automatic approval. Business credit ranges from 0 to 100, with the median score for the childcare business industry, hovering around an 89. Childcare centers often pay debt within terms, but they're held back by the industry business failure score. In which childcare businesses fail at an alarming rate. This failure rate is referred as the industry rating risk. In addition, the childcare industry is associated with having tax liens, judgements, and business bankruptcy in comparison to other related industries. When applying for credit accounts, you may receive a denial that reads, "high industry rating risk". If you're denied for this reason, the only thing you can do as an owner is to strengthen your credit profile by allowing it to age. In order to lower the risk, the industry has to change as a whole. It's not only what you and I contribute but all childcare business owners together. If you really want the account you could ask for a smaller limit, be a personal guarantor, or place a deposit. Note: Even though you're a personal guarantor, it doesn't mean the creditor will report to the personal credit bureau. It just means that you're ultimately responsible for paying back the debt if the account is closed with a balance or the business files bankruptcy and creditor is listed.

Credit References

Business credit references are essentially information about the business that can provide details about the business's past track record with credit. Creditors and the business banking institution may provide credit references for businesses. Credit references provide factual information with your consent, so that a creditor can make a decision about whether to lend you money. Keep in mind that traditionally, a creditor may re-check references if an established business customer begins to reveal signs of financial troubles or changes its payment or buying pattern. If the business Paydex score declines significantly, it's not uncommon for the creditor to restrict account access or even close the account.

Type of trade references to add to your account:

1. Trade References should be companies who have extended you credit on terms, have invoiced you, and have received payment back from you within those terms (Net 30, net 60, 45 days, etc.).

2. Do not use companies who automatically debit a payment from a credit card or checking account.

3. You can use any invoiced service paid in the past 45 days to 12 months.

4. They do not need to be constant (monthly) charges but can be one- time invoiced purchases.

5. Very large companies are likely to be automatic reporters with D&B, but there is no way of knowing if they are or are not. Just submit the trade reference and see if they are declined (or ask your vendor).

**** If a reference is declined for "Attempts Exhausted" and you see the option to "re-submit", it means they were declined because there was insufficient data. Gather better contact info and resubmit. ****

10 Examples of the type of vendors to add that could qualify as references:

(Think about who you've paid in the last 12 months)

1. Website design

2. Uniform Supplier

3. Lawyer

4. Accountant

5. Office Furniture Rental

6. Display Equipment

7. Warehouse Rental

8. Refuse/Garbage/Dumpster Rental/Waste Management (not associated with your municipality)

9. Marketing company

10. Direct Mail Service

Examples of Questions Vendors Will Be Asked When D&B Calls Them:

1. How long you have been doing business with them
2. Their line of business and what type of service they provide to you
3. Highest invoice amount ever on file
4. Most recent invoice dates
5. What kinds of terms they give you - Net 30, 10net30, COD
6. How do you pay - prompt, slow, prepaid, etc.
7. Who they are talking to, their position, their callback number (must be corporate)

There are 4 main reasons why D&B will decline a reference.

1. The company automatically reports all of their transactions to D&B
2. The company is not a US company
3. The company does not have an established D&B credit file
4. The company is a bank, charge account, credit card, or utility

D&B Declined References

1. Unsuccessfully contact after attempting six times
2. The company has been declared a higher risk company
3. The company is on the Do Not Call list
4. Company policy prohibits reporting credit experiences
5. Company's callback number is not the corporate number.

There is no way of knowing why a trade reference was declined by D&B, but if a trade reference is declined due to the reason "automatically reports all of their transactions to D&B", the information may still end up on your report, so long as that company has your DUNS number on file when they report.

Need a credit reference? Try Strategic Networks. Credit references can be given by this company in order to acquire larger accounts with other major businesses. Strategic Networks issues credit references through Dun and Bradstreet.

UCC Filings

UCC stands for uniform commercial code, which means it's a code that oversees the sale of leased goods. There are two main types. Oftentimes, with business, UCC-1 is associated. It's a claim on a specific asset or assets. UCC Filings are filed with the secretary of state and have their own section on D&B reports. For example, I leased a high-valued printer, thinking the lease agreement would be reported as business credit. The printer was worth approximately $4,000. Over the next two years, I got free ink, free maintenance, and free technical support, in addition to the printer. The printing company filed a UCC for usage and customary filing. That filing was reported to D & B. The value is not listed but all the company information is. The company essentially says, we have interest in this business, so if this business is bankrupt, we have some stake in this object. I couldn't sell the printer to settle debts if the business goes bankrupt. If you have a UCC filing, make sure it's current at all times. Check for duplicates as well. Whenever the term is up, be sure to get a copy of the release and request the release to be submitted to the secretary of state.

Credit Card Options

Capital One Spark Card (bronze-colored card)

Capital One will place a hard pull on your Transunion credit report. You must have a credit score of 600 to qualify and current positive accounts within the last six months. They report to only your personal credit file. You must give a personal guarantee. It will be reported to your consumer credit file, not your business file.

Wells Fargo Secured Credit Card

Wells Fargo will place a hard pull on your consumer Equifax credit report. If you have collections, it's an automatic denial. But, once established, Wells Fargo will report to your Experian Business Credit File. No personal guarantee is necessary, but it requires an initial deposit of $500.00 or more for the card. It's possible for you to graduate to a regular business credit card after a year of positive payments and no over-the-limit transactions. If you have a decent credit score above 600, you don't have any collections, and you don't have too many outstanding inquiries, then you can try for the Wells Fargo business card. If you don't qualify, you can still get the secured card, for which you just have to put

$500 down, and you're automatically approved. When I was building my credit, I drove 120 miles to my nearest Wells Fargo in Indiana to make sure that I got the Wells Fargo secured business card. They report to Experian every month. Keep your balance low, pay it on time, just like any other credit card, and ensure it is in your business' name.

THE BIZ CREDIT CLEAN UP

**Repairing, Restoring, or
Reusing the Business Credit Profile**

We've all been there, where we've utilized our credit to bail us out of temporary situations. The problem is that the temporary situation turns into a bigger one, and we're left to clean up the mess. Oftentimes, the situation ends in a tax lien, collections, business bankruptcy, or even worse, business closure. The good news is that once you develop your "get out of jail" free card, then you've officially freed yourself and the burden you've carried. Every person has a unique situation which requires a unique game plan. Let me take you behind the curtain at Rivers once more and dive deeper into my huge loss with a huge gain.

Last year, I decided my goal was to expand to another center. I was hesitant. I didn't let anybody convince me to go get a second center until I was ready. I knew that I had to have my personal credit in line. I knew I had to have my business credit in line. So, I went into research mode.

Every month, I tracked my creditors – who was reporting, who wasn't. I got on the phone, I called every creditor, I tracked it each and every month. I also had the help of a friend. She asked, "Why are you doing this?" I replied, "Because I know that I need for my business credit." And I also knew I needed money in order to do that. So, I took my profits from my current center, and I was able to secure $34,000 in SBA funding from an outside source. To secure funding, they drilled me, they looked at my LinkedIn profile, they researched my Facebook friends, they looked at my Instagram account. And still, I was able to acquire funding, but I had to have those things set up. I even had my staff help me mail letters to clean up my personal credit. We were all on a mission for success.

What I failed to realize during that point was the status of all of my other stuff. By stuff I mean, the smaller debts that weren't urgent or had longer Net Terms. I had a substantial amount of personal debt accumulated, and then my overhead increased tenfold. I went from writing 6 to 7 hundred-dollar checks to 6/7 thousand dollars at a time for a property that wasn't mine. Even the team I chose had become watered down and costly. At round 3 of the business credit building process, it requires less involvement of the personal credit and more so business credit history. It's heavily weighted on longevity of the business credit profile. It's a game of company age and size.

Once I possessed a high Paydex score, 10+ reporting tradelines, and personal credit in good standing, I was able to acquire the funding needed for my next level. No personal credit check, only the business information. Afterwards, I was able to negotiate my own specific repayment terms. The power had shifted, my business was now established and operating at a new level. I sat in front of investors whom told me their vision for my childcare center. They told me, "We've got the right business, and we've got the right business owner." It felt great to pierce the ceiling and have resources at my disposal but with great power comes great responsibility.

Through the process of expansion, a plan B, C, and D should always be in the works. As quickly as my dream center was established, it quickly fell. I was devastated. The state went through a big transition and it ultimately put me in a bind. When a huge emergency happened, and it did – the ceiling came crashing down – I wasn't prepared. My landlord was supposed to be responsible, but he went MIA because he was cash-flow broke as well. Therefore, I had nobody to lean on, other than my attorney. My attorney was the key factor to get me out of "jail" without paying for the 5-year contract. Even though, I no longer had a lease, my business was in a state of financial crisis. Broken agreements, Debt Beyond Terms, returned payroll checks, and most of all a broken spirit. But I survived an $80,000 loss in January 2018 and bounced back to purchase a property in October 2018 for $100,000. Experiencing that loss had me scared straight. I was afraid to make decisions as a CEO, if I had the same mentality in January, as today, I could've a lot further. Sometimes decisions are all in the way you frame them.

Make your foundation solid BEFORE trying to expand. Use my 3-C's of business which are Credit, Cash-flow, and Cash On-Hand. Ensure that cash is steadily flowing through the business. You've established business credit with at least 5 tradelines and 2 business credit cards, and a minimum of $10,000 cash on-hand. You can't really prepare for what the state does, but you do have the power and control to make sure that your business will last through the changes or at least overcome 90 to 120 days without receiving any additional money from the state. Prepare for that. Learn from my credit story.

Maxing Out Credit Limits

This won't hurt your score too much, as long as you're within terms. Go beyond terms and that does most of the damage. Pay early and the creditor may give you a credit line increase. Business credit doesn't have the same negative effect as personal credit when going above 30% of the credit line. It's simply an indicator that you want to do more business with the creditor. A credit line increase usually takes 2-3 months after opening the account.

Liens

A lien, is a lien, is a lien. It doesn't matter if it's an IRS lien, or if it's a maintenance lien. IRS liens automatically affect your Paydex score. It doesn't matter how many trade payments you have recorded there. It doesn't matter how many credit cards you have reported there. Your business credit score will be affected. My Paydex score automatically dropped down to a 42 due to a tax lien. For lack of better words, you've got a couple of options: pay it, negotiate a settlement with the help of a tax attorney, or close the business and reopen another one in a different industry.

Judgements/Collections

Judgements and collections work the same way as personal credit, but they're much harder to get deleted from the business credit profile. If you can negotiate a settlement without going to court or collections, try that route instead.

Bankruptcy

Business bankruptcy is a beast. For all owners who are set up as sole proprietors, this is the reason you may not want to structure your business as such. If your business goes bankrupt, your business is an extension of you. There isn't any separation between the business assets and your personal assets. All debts will be tied to you regardless. The owner is responsible for all assets and liabilities. Business bankruptcy can be handled in two additional ways, which are Chapter 7, in which the business in the foreseeable future ceases to exist, the assets are dissolved, and the bankruptcy court takes possession. Or, Chapter 11, which is a reorganization of debt in which creditors, the bankruptcy court, and partners/corporations come to an agreement for repayment. This is an option if the business has a future. Note, Chapter 13 could be filed for sole proprietors once a detailed plan for repayment has been established.

Also note, if the business is still in operation, you'll want to keep utilizing open credit lines to maintain the credit history. Do not go overboard or spend any extra time or money on needless items. Purchase only what the business needs during this time. If you plan to make a major comeback, know it's possible but work the plan.

PROTECTING THE BUSINESS

Credit Privacy Numbers

Once you've successfully completed the credit building process, it would be a shame if the fate of the business lay in the hands of a deceitful person. If you feel that your business information has been exposed. Or you feel someone has committed business identity fraud. You could apply for a Credit Privacy Number also known as a CPN. CPN's are usually associated with consumer credit profiles. By having a CPN, it would add an extra layer of protection but do not expect fast turn-arounds for credit decisions. Lenders aren't required to use CPN's so weigh your options. The best way to keep track is through credit monitoring. In addition, always notify business credit agencies if identity theft has occurred, a fraud alert will display on the business credit profile.

Secure All Business Sensitive Files

Safeguard all business-related information. These documents are your business birth certificate or the articles of organization and social security card of the Tax Id Number. These files cannot be thrown around loosely because someone could use them and operate another business around yours. According to the United States Attorney's Office, "In 2014, an employee at Builder's Supply Source, Inc., a cabinetry supply company in Nashville, Tenn. Was a victim of business identity theft. A former employee was arrested after being indicted by a federal grand jury on charges of bank fraud, wire fraud and identity theft. According to the indictment, between May 2014 and October 2016, the former employee was employed as the office manager and bookkeeper.

The indictment alleges that the employee used their position to make fraudulent charges to American Express credit cards issued to company employees, utilizing the mobile payment application Square, Inc. The employee renamed their account with Square to closely resemble the name of a legitimate vendor and then used Square to process cash transfers to the personal bank account. During this execution of this scheme, the employee made fraudulent transfers 289 times that totaled more than $500,000."

Check Out Vendor Information

Check out vendor profiles before doing business. As a business owner you have the ability to conduct research on other businesses that you'll work with. You can acquire this information on the D&B website which furnishes information on other businesses. You'll be able figure out if a vendor is credible, reliable, and a legitimate business. Doing business with businesses that aren't registered, filed bankruptcy, or has numerous tax liens is risky business. For example, after purchasing the property for our new center, I had to find businesses to perform jobs such as installing plumbing. Typically, a landlord would help with this process and has built relationships with other businesses. However, I chose to use enter into an agreement with a plumber that had done work for me before. Not following the process of doing background check, left me exposed. I paid a deposit and the plumber went MIA. Not only was my money gone but I had to get another plumber to perform the job. In order to get my money returned I have to sue the owner and his company. In addition, his license had expired, and he lacked insurance. When you level-up, automatically assume, that you'll need a new team in order to handle the job. If you reuse the same individuals or businesses, reassess their background information, business practices, and ask for references.

Check Invoices & Statements

Check invoices and statements frequently. Checking these items frequently, decreases the opportunity of identity theft, reveals employee misuse of credit cards, and also reveals company waste. The Builder's Supply case could've been prevented if credit monitoring was intact. Alerts are sent directly to the business owner about accounts created, changed, or closed. In addition, merchant accounts are also monitored. If you can afford D & B's business all-inclusive package, it's a great asset. It's designed for larger companies that don't have the time to watch over their business credit profiles.

Copyright & Trademark Materials

Copyright and trademark everything that's unique to your business. Both protects intellectual property protection, but copyrights protect literature and videos whole trademarks protects items attached to a brand, such as a logo. Trademarks may also protect words, phrases, symbols, or other devices. To register a copyright or trademark, start by visiting the U.S. Patent and Trademark Office's Web site, www.uspto.gov. If you need assistance reach out to a patent/trademark attorney.

Always remember you are the business' first line of defense with proper business setup. You're also the business last line of defense because no one will care about your business as much as you do. Fail to provide proper nourishment and guidance by getting the knowledge for growth, could mean a closure of business operations. Even though you can start another business, never go down without a fight.

CLOSING REMARKS

I really want to put the odds in childcare business owners' favor. We're sitting in a spot where we're at a disadvantage. Even when you apply for your Dun and Bradstreet number, our industry rating is high risk immediately. The odds are against you as soon as you create your credit profile. When I started my business credit for the childcare industry, my approved credit was only $500. But when I started my consulting business, my automatic approval was $7500. What a difference. A $7,000 difference because of the industry that I'm working in.

If that's the difference with childcare, imagine with other industries. Again, as a childcare business owner, the odds are against us. I'm here to help put the odds in your favor so we can all go from point A to point B, and we can make quality childcare centers while ensuring that we can stand on a solid financial foundation.

We shouldn't have to keep going through the same challenges. We're not going to let history repeat itself. Our industry has to change altogether. I'm here to help. All the struggles that I went through, I'm glad to have experienced. It gives me the opportunity to share the wealth of information along to other business owners.

In closing, I hope that this book gave you the boost needed to get you on the right track for success in your childcare business. Our industry is one that needs the knowledge of business to overcome forces working against us. Through this book, I leave my personal credit journey as well as my business credit journey. If you didn't get enough and need further help, try coaching with me. You won't be disappointed. Until next time. Let's get to the money.

CREDITS & REFERENCES

"Ashland City Woman Facing Federal Charges For Credit Card Fraud." The United States Department of Justice, 14 Aug. 2017, www.justice.gov/usao-mdtn/pr/ashland-city-woman-facing-federal-charges-credit-card-fraud.

Business Finance
https://www.thebalancesmb.com/what-is-business-bankruptcy-393017

Collection Shield 360
https://www.collectionshield360.com

D & B
https://www.dnb.com

Equifax Small Business
https://sb.econsumer.equifax.com/bizdirect/companySearch.ehtml?advancedSearch=true

Experian Small Business
http://www.experian.com/small-business/services.jsp

NAV
https://www.nav.com/blog/ucc-filings-and-business-credit-scores-8189/

United States Census Bureau
https://www.census.gov/eos/www/naics/

United States Patent and Trademark Office
www.uspto.gov

ABOUT THE AUTHOR

Asia L. Rivers is the owner and operator of Rivers Educational Center and CEO of Talk Childcare To Me. Mrs. Rivers services an average of 50 families, providing a safe, nurturing and progressive facility for children aged six weeks to 13 years. Rivers Educational Center continues to make strides by giving children access to quality education and nutritional meals, delivered by highly trained staff members who share a common goal of excellence. Asia holds an undergraduate degree in Psychology and recently obtained her Childcare Director's Credential and ECE Trainer's Credential, which has expanded her knowledge in supervising staff, overseeing daily activities, designing curriculums, and preparing budgets. The knowledge she has obtained from college, graduate school, and her own foster care experiences has been advantageous in her journey to building a childcare empire. Asia's energy, passion, and dedication for today's children are apparent in her daily mission to own and maintain the best childcare facility in Louisville, Ky. Over the last two years, Asia has obtained nearly $100,000 in funding from national entities, crowdfunding efforts, federal agencies, and statewide organizations that support her vision. Asia has used her grant funds and loans for classroom makeovers, purchasing quality materials, building expansions, and hiring initiatives. Her immediate goal and priority is to increase awareness by coaching childcare businessowners to build business credit. She teaches them how to establish resilience in the business world. She spends her time advocating for children in her state and advocating for higher reimbursement rates for childcare providers. When Asia isn't overseeing 12 staff members and an average of 50 children, she enjoys spending quality time at home with her husband William and 5 children. In addition, she is a self-published author of The Talk Childcare To Me series.

GET TO THE MONEY AND TAKE ADVANTAGE OF ONE ON ONE COACHING

Website URL: wwww.talkchildcaretome.com

Facebook: Asia Rivers, Talk Childcare To Me

Facebook Group: Talk Childcare and Business Credit

Instagram: BizCreditBae

Twitter: _BizCreditGuru

LinkedIn: Asia L. Rivers

email: info@talkbizcredit.com

Made in the USA
Middletown, DE
18 January 2019